NORWEGIAN MUSIC AND COMPOSERS

Part of the manuscript of Grieg's song *The Swan* set to words
by Henrik Ibsen   [*Frontispiece*

NORWEGIAN MUSIC AND COMPOSERS

by

BÖRRE QVAMME

LONDON

THE BOND PUBLISHING COMPANY

FIRST PUBLISHED APRIL 1949

780.948
Qv 9n

35619
November, 1957

Printed in Great Britain by
THE NAROD PRESS, LONDON, E.1

Distributed by
HANDEL SMITHY & CO. LTD.
395 EDGWARE ROAD, LONDON, W.2

CONTENTS

ILLUSTRATIONS

CHAPTER 1

FOLK MUSIC

NORWAY is one of those countries which for centuries had no outlet for her artistic genius other than folk art. After the decay of the Norwegian monarchy in the 14th century, Norway had neither a court nor an aristocracy or a wealthy middle class which could foster national art. With the downfall of the Norwegian Catholic Church and the abolition of the Archbishopric of Trondheim the last institution was gone that stood for national independence and could give opportunities to Norwegian artists. For five centuries the Norwegians were ruled from Copenhagen, capital of Denmark, which attracted the best that Norway possessed in artistic or scientific talent. Only with the re-establishment of an independent Norwegian State in 1814, could the foundations for a free development of literary and artistic activities be laid.

The result of these conditions was that nearly all music produced in Norway right up to the 19th century was anonymous folk music, handed down, through the ages, from father to son. Not till the 19th century were the songs and dances of the Norwegian peasants written down; representing, as they did, the main fund of the nation's musical tradition, it is natural that folk music has had a relatively greater importance in Norway than e.g. in Britain, France, Italy or Germany. The rise of Norwegian music in art-form coincided with the national romantic movements in Europe, with the birth of Czech, Polish, Hungarian and Russian music. In that period Norwegian composers consciously sought to adapt their own musical idiom to that of the popular tradition. International art-forms like the sonata, the concerto and the symphony were adopted, but filled with material gathered from folk music; traditional ballads and dance tunes, in particular, were decisively influencing the work of creative musicians. No work on Norwegian music can, therefore, ignore the anonymous folk music into which the creative genius of Norway poured its soul for centuries.

Racially and culturally the Norwegians are a fairly homogeneous nation. No great invasions are known to have taken place for 2,000 years, and the composition of the population has changed little since the Bronze Age. The Norwegians are, scientifically speaking, mainly fair-haired dolichocephalic Nordics speaking a Germanic language, and their closest relations are the Danes and the Swedes. One may safely say that up to the Viking Age there were no marked differences between the Scandinavian peoples either in culture or in language, and therefore information obtained on the basis of archeological investigation in one country can be easily complemented with material obtained from other areas.

The earliest information we possess about the music of the Scandinavians is supplied by the finds of Bronze Age horns. More than twenty of them have been found in Denmark, eight in Sweden and two in Norway. As only one specimen was located outside Scandinavia (in Northern Germany), they seem to have been peculiar to Northern Europe. These instruments are masterpieces of craftsmanship and must have been most impressive both in appearance and in tone. As they are often found in pairs (which by their symmetrical construction show that they were probably used simultaneously) it is likely that the Scandinavian peoples knew some kind of harmony already in the Bronze Age.

However that may be, the Scandinavians showed marked predilection for singing in parts when they next appeared in musical history, in the Viking Age. We have the evidence of Giraldus Cambrensis who, in his *Descriptio Cambriæ,* mentions that people in the North of England sing in two-part harmony, which according to him is a Danish heritage. But neither in Denmark nor in Sweden or Norway are there any traces of singing in harmony, though in Iceland, which has preserved old traditions better than other Scandinavian countries, two- or three-part singing has been common for centuries. We find references to the so-called *tvisyngja* (two-part singing) in medieval literature, and the opposition of the Church to part-singing suggests that it was a popular practice which went back to pre-Christian times. These facts seem to support Fétis's theory that singing in harmony originated in the North, and it is also possible that the major-minor scale—detested by strict Church musicians—was developed among the peoples of the North of Europe. The old Icelandic melodies seem to follow no scale whatever, but the frequent progression by thirds in Nordic melodies would naturally lead to the formation of the major and minor chord.

But even if the supposition were true that Northern music naturally tended towards major-minor harmonies, Church music could not avoid influencing the music of the people. The Gregorian chants, following the oriental modes or the modes of medieval theorists, subtly changed the musical taste of the people. Of the Norwegian folk songs collected in the last century a surprisingly large number show characteristics peculiar to plain-song, such as modal cadences and melismata. The Lydian scale with its augmented fourth is a favourite in Norwegian folk music, and in quite a number of folk songs the semitone is avoided as a leading tone. Very often a vacillation is noticeable between a whole tone and a semitone, and both may be found in different variants of the same melody. But it is impossible to say whether the semitone is a later influence from European art music or whether it is original or whether, finally, the whole leading tone is due to the influence of the Roman Catholic plain-song.

In any case, Christian church music was accepted whole-heartedly and soon became a part of the musical consciousness of the people. In sagas and chronicles there are several references to the beautiful singing in the church and its great effect on the people. Norwegian church music developed characteristics of its own just as it was the case in other European countries, and new melodies were composed for special Norwegian services. Some of these are preserved in incomplete manuscripts, as many of these priceless parchment sheets were, in later centuries, used for binding accounts and reports. Nearly all the music which has been preserved relates to the St. Olav Mass sung at the Cathedral of Trondheim (Nidaros) in honour of the

patron saint of Norway. Although this material has not yet
been thoroughly examined, most of the neumes have been
transcribed by Dr. Georg Reiss, and some of the hymns
have found their way into the new prayer book of the
Lutheran Church of Norway.

Between the 14th and the 18th centuries no music was
recorded in Norway, so we are unable to follow the course
of its development. However, different phases can be distinguished in the mass of folk songs and dances collected
since 1800. Because of the subject matter and linguistic
peculiarities the epic ballads must be acknowledged as its
oldest element and the tunes they were sung to have probably changed little since the poems were composed in the
14th and 15th centuries. These ballads were preserved for
four or five centuries in the isolated valleys of Setesdal and
Telemark and new melodies were composed, modelled on
the old ones, to the Danish folk ballads, collected and
published by Peder Syv in the 16th century. Syv's work
circulated in Norway and gave rise both to new tunes and
new poems. Musical activity in these far-off parts of
Norway must have been considerable as several entirely
different tunes are preserved for the very same texts.

The ballad tunes bear the stamp of great antiquity. They
are forceful, striking and in keeping with the intensely
dramatic text. For centuries Norwegian people danced to
the music of these dramas in the long winter evenings.
Their innumerable verses were usually sung by one of the
oldsters gifted with a specially good memory, and the rest
joined in the refrain. At the time the ballads were collected
and noted down, the dances were all but forgotten. But
in the Faroe Islands, linguistically and culturally part
of Norway, though politically Danish since 1814, people
still dance to the interminable epic ballads about giants,
monsters, heroes and great lovers. The steps used are
always the same : the couples hold each other by the arm
and form a circle which moves in and out in loops towards
the centre, and there is something monotonous in the un-
varying rhythm and movement. But this very monotony
grows exciting as the dance progresses; the movement in a
body to age-old rhythms and to the singing of stirring
tales has something electrifying about it. In these isolated

islands ballad dancing is still the chief entertainment and shows no signs of dying out.

A few of the ballads have religious subjects; such is the theme of the greatest of all folk poems, the ancient ballad about the *Vision of Heaven and Hell* (*Draumkvedet*). This is a Dantesque poem about a man who in his sleep visits the world of the dead to see the damned and the saints and the Last Judgment. Both words and music are very impressive, and by their modal cadences the melodies give the impression of great age. They were certainly inspired by the music heard in the churches in the pre-Reformation period. But many of the heroic ballads show similar characteristics; church modes are as frequent as the major and minor scale. As several of these tunes must have been composed after plain-song has been abolished in the Lutheran churches, they are a proof that the musical taste of those parts of the country was still under the influence of the modal church music.

Another body of folk tunes strengthens the impression that church modes, i.e. hymn tunes, were dear to the Norwegians. Hymn-singing was introduced by the Reformation and new hymns were constantly being composed by poet-preachers. Luther himself took the melodies of the people and used them for his religious hymns, and new tunes had been composed by his musical friends. These chorales differed from the Roman Catholic plain-song which was still partly used in the Lutheran service. When new hymn-books arrived in Norway from Denmark, people spontaneously made up new tunes to sing them to. Whenever German or Danish tunes were introduced, they were changed out of all recognition. As these tunes travelled from one part of the country to the other and altered in the process, they can be found in many variants. The result is an astonishing profusion of hymn-tunes all over Norway; they were taken down by the hundreds by interested collectors. Some of them have the character of plain-song with their chantlike cadences and rich melismata. When the original German chorales were taught to the peasants, they were embellished with similar grace notes and the cadences were changed to conform to modal practice.

Although Norwegian hymn tunes often give an impression of great age, most of them must have been composed in the 17th and 18th centuries. The favourite hymn books were those of BISHOP KINGO (1634-1703) and BISHOP BRORSON (1694-1764). The latter's forceful and sensuous poetry especially, inspired some of the most beautiful of Norwegian religious music. During the religious revival of the 18th century these hymns became the daily bread of most Norwegian; until supplanted by religious tunes from Britain and America in the latter part of the 19th century, they were the only music not considered sinful. The religious revival created a Puritan spirit in many parts of the country; there grew as its effect an opposition to amusements, and dancing and secular music were placed in the same category of sinful pursuits as play-acting or card-playing.

The epic ballads and the hymn-tunes are perhaps the most valuable and the most significant elements of Norwegian folk music. Their beauty of outline, their expressiveness and depth of feeling raises them to the rank of great music in spite of their limitations. That music contains many other interesting aspects. Already in the 12th and 13th centuries lyric poetry made its appearance with short verses interpolated in the sagas. When the epic period of folk literature came to an end, Norwegian poets turned to love and nature for inspiration. The art of composing short lyrical poems continued almost up to the present day, and lyric folk poetry may therefore date from the 15th to the 19th centuries. The music set to the shorter lyrics will therefore offer a variety of styles, but generally speaking, it has a more modern character.

Setesdal, the most conservative of all Norwegian valleys, preserved its medieval character both in art, dress, manners and mental outlook far into the 19th century, and it is there that we find the *stev,* a peculiar kind of improvised lyrics. The *stev* was always composed on the same metrical pattern and to the same melodies, and at large gatherings one of the chief amusements was the composition of new verses on the accepted patterns. It was a competition in wit and poetry which took the form of bandying the *stev* from person to person. Declarations of love, praise of nature, satiric descriptions of people and places, banter between boys and girls—were all set in the same metre to the old traditional tunes. In other parts of the country, poems were composed freely and set to original music. The themes were the same as everywhere else in the world : descriptions of the beloved, lamentation of an unrequitted love, lullabies, nonsense songs and nursery rhymes, the usual ingredients of the greater part of lyrical poetry. The music is often of great beauty, though the songs have none of the wiry strength and direct forcefulness of the epic ballads. They are softer and sweeter and their melodic line is more modern in character.

Lyrical songs are found all over the country, but the ballads were only preserved in far-off valleys like Setesdal, Telemark, Hallingdal and Valdres. Often the words had already been forgotten when the melodies were taken down, or the singers would have only nonsense words to fit the tune. Sometimes new words were added to old ballad tunes; a very fine melody known as the *Ravens' Wedding in Crow Wood* has thus been preserved until today.

There is no doubt that many of the old songs were already forgotten when folk-lorists took to collecting folk music in the 1840's. Only a handful of folk songs were noted down before Lindemann published his fine collection between 1840 and 1867. But there was enough left to show the inventiveness and musical genius of the people, and as layer after layer was isolated, a rough idea could be obtained of the development of Norwegian music through the centuries.

New tunes were still being composed when Lindemann started collecting folk music about 1840 and some of the most popular melodies were of fairly recent origin. Songs like *Astri, mi Astri* and the satirical ditty *Paul on the Hill* were, in fact, so new that attempts had been made to determine the names of their writers or composers. By that time the influence of classical and romantic music, of operatic airs and foreign dance music made itself felt, and the most recent folk tunes had, therefore, an entirely modern character. The church modes were forgotten, and only in far-off districts did musical taste still tend towards augmented fourths (the Lydian mode) and the whole-step leading tone. The new tunes were in the major or minor scale and were, generally, less distinguished than the old ones.

The new dances introduced during the Renaissance (15th and 16th centuries) entirely supplanted ballad dancing so that no vestiges of them were left except in the Faroe Islands. In fact, all dances now connected with folk songs were created in more recent times by individuals interested in the revival of the old song-dance. The oldest of the authentic Norwegian dances is probably the *halling*, an acrobatic solo dance for men, not unlike the Cossack dance. The music is in 2/4 time, perhaps the most characteristic Norwegian dance music. Norwegian composers have often used the *halling* rhythm in their compositions.

For centuries the most popular dance was the *springar* or *springdans*, several variants of which are still popular in a number of country districts. The music is always in 3/4 time, but the rhythm varies. The three beats may be equal as in a waltz, or the second may be stressed as in a *mazurka*, or, finally, the third beat may be stressed (Röros-*springar*, Gudbrandsdal-*springar*, Telemark-*springar*). Its origin can be traced to the German *Springtanz* of the 16th century; its companion the *Gangtanz* was introduced to Norway as *gangar*. All through Renaissance Europe a slow dance was followed by a quick dance, the *pavan* by the *allemand* or the *galliard*, the *Gangtanz* by the *Springtanz*, and in Norway this pair became the *gangar* and the *springar*. The slower *gangar* in 2/4 or 6/8 time has now been forgotten except in Setesdal, but the *springar* is fairly common. Both these dances play a great part both in folk and in art-form music; there are many examples of the *springar* in the works of Grieg and Johan Svendsen.

These dances were either played on the German violin or the Norwegian *hardingfele* which has four sympathetic strings under the usual four strings. The tuning may vary from one musical piece to the other. The vibration of the sympathetic strings gives to the tune a sonorous accompaniment of fourths and fifths like the skirl of a bagpipe; an open fifths of the harmony has become a characteristic of all Norwegian music and is very frequent in Grieg's piano pieces. The *hardingfele* is, however, confined to certain districts, like Hardanger, Voss, Telemark and Hallingdal. In other parts the ordinary violin has triumphed. In Valdres the *langeleik* is played up to the present day. The *langeleik* resembles a zither with one melody string and seven open strings used for the accompaniment; it produces a pleasant tinkling tone. The fourth national instrument is the *seljeflöyte*, a flute made out of a willow branch.

Although slowly, European fashions in dress, art and music made their way from the large towns, through the surrounding country districts, to the farthest fjords and mountain valleys. Likewise, the 18th century dances spread from the halls of the wealthy *bourgeoisie* to peasant farms, while sailors introduced popular dances from Holland, England and Scotland. Most foreign dances were altered and new ones created on their model and, today, Norway can boast of a great variety of dances of the country type : the *figaro*, the *fandango* (which has nothing in common with the Spanish dance), the *aattetur* (an eightsome reel) and *sekstur* (reel), the *reinlender*, etc. The music played to these dances is often still recognizably Scotch or English. Later still the *waltz*, the *mazurka* and the *polka* appeared and are still most popular in many country districts. Folk dance music composed during the last hundred years belongs mostly to the *waltz*, *reinlender* (from German *Rheinländer*, a dance in 2/4 time) or *mazurka* type and is mostly played on the accordion or the fiddle. Many folk dance societies, however, make an effort to keep up the interest in the *springar*, the various country dances and the modern song-dances performed to the tune of the old folk songs.

Districts like Telemark have remained true to the *hardingfele* and the making and playing of this instrument became a highly developed art. Fiddlers using this instrument did not only play dance music and marches at bridal processions, but often gave solo pieces as a concert performance. Thus originated the *slaatt*, at first a march-like tune played on the *fele* which soon developed into a character piece. Grieg's transcriptions of folk music for the piano contain several examples of *slaatter*.

The epic ballads as well as religious hymns, lyrical songs, cradle songs and nursery rhymes, dances and the *slaatter* make up the great bulk of the Norwegian folk music. Here, too, belong occupational songs—songs and calls used by dairy maids to call the cattle home, bits of melodies played on the horn like the Swiss *Ranz des vaches,* ditties used in connection with work or play. Some of the cow calls are musically very interesting and show an extensive use of the interval of the seventh.

The earliest recorded piece of Norwegian folk music is a *halling* dating back to 1695; otherwise nothing had appeared in print before Laborde's publication of several Norwegian songs in his *Essais sur la musique ancienne et moderne* (Paris 1780). Although Danish musicologists like Nyerup, Rahbek and Berggreen did include some Norwegian melodies in their collections, it was only in the middle of the 19th century that the first extensive collection of Norwegian folk music was brought out. It was edited by Ludvig Mathias Lindemann, who published 636 numbers in all. But more than 1,000 pieces are still in manuscript at the University Library of Oslo. At the turn of the century Catharinus Elling started collecting folk music, but only a fraction of his records has, so far, been published. The third great collector of folk music was O. M. Sandvik who confined his activities mainly to Eastern Norway. Both Elling and Sandvik wrote valuable works on the Norwegian folk music. The composer Johan Halvorsen collected a large number of *slaatter* and his work was continued by A. Björndal who published several books of *slaatter* for the fiddle. Although a number of other workers were active in this field the collections of Lindeman, Elling, Sandvik, Halvorsen and Björndal continue to be regarded as standard reference works. They are also the most readily available publications of this kind in Norway.

CHAPTER 2

THE NATIONAL REVIVAL

THERE is no need to emphasize the extremely provincial character of Norwegian culture up to the 19th century. In conditions prevailing in the 17th and 18th centuries only a court could afford to sponsor a theatre, an opera or a large *ensemble* of musicians. Consequently Norway had none of these. There was no *grand seigneur* like Esterhazy, no music-loving princes and counts who could support a Haydn or a Beethoven. The towns were small, and the petty middle class too pre-occupied with earning a livelihood to care for the finer arts. What music was needed was supplied by fiddlers, trumpeters and oboists who, as occasion demanded, played minuets and *springars* at the burgomaster's ball, or sang chorales from the church tower on Easter morning. The chief towns usually had some officially appointed town players, led by the Town Musician, who was given the privilege of licensing all musicians in his district. Often these Town Musicians combined their job with a conspicuously non-musical occupation such as that of a chief of the fire brigade, manager of the water-works, etc.; usually they were organists as well.

Several of these Town Musicians, who generally occupied an honoured position and enjoyed enviable rights and privileges, were immigrants from Germany and had a solid foundation in music. Such was the Town Musician of Trondheim, JOHAN DANIEL BERLIN (died in 1787). His son JOHAN HEINRICH BERLIN (1741—1807), had real talent and composed symphonies, concertos for harpsichord and for horn, string quartets and cantatas in the style of the times. His symphonies were scored for strings, two oboes, a bassoon and two horns. A great number of his manuscripts are preserved in the library of the Royal Society of Sciences in Trondheim, but none of them has been published.

As the *bourgeoisie* of the 18th century grew in wealth and position, it found more and more opportunity for cultivating the arts. This was especially the case with Oslo, which was the administrative centre of the country and the residence of several important officials, including the Viceroy. In 1749 the people of Oslo had, on the occasion of a royal visit, the opportunity of hearing an Italian operatic troupe with Christoph Willibald Gluck as maestro. Later on, musical societies were formed in Bergen, Oslo and Trondheim. The first of them, founded in 1775 and known as the *Harmonien,* is the oldest phil-harmonic society of Norway. At that time orchestras were composed of both professional musicians and interested amateurs; they gave public concerts regularly, but their programmes would now probably be found to be in ques-tionable taste. Towards the end of the century a brisk musical life developed in the homes of the wealthy, and the importance of this movement for the future of Norway's musical culture can scarcely be overestimated. Many of the most prominent musicians of later periods, Thrane, Ole Bull, Kjerulf, Grieg and Selmer, came from this class of merchants and State officials.

The war of 1807-14 proved a set-back to the arts, as most of the rich families were ruined in the great financial crisis which followed it. On the other hand, Norway became a sovereign State, and Oslo's rise to the status of a nation's capital meant that some effort at providing cultural life, worthy of an independent nation, had to be made. But as Norway had formed a personal union with Sweden and the King continued to reside in Stockholm, Oslo (or Christiania, as it was then called) could not boast of a court, and the poverty of the country set strict limits to its artistic ambitions. The musical life of the capital was con-sequently still very provincial. The community could not support many musicians, and a real artist had great diffi-culty in maintaining himself. There was a musical society which arranged the performances of Haydn and Mozart symphonies or provided accompanists to violin concertos of Viotti, Kreutzer, Rode and Spohr and to the piano con-certos of Mozart, Dussek, Gyrowetz and Clementi when-ever these were played. At the dramatic society the musical comedies of Boïeldieu, d'Alayrac and Devienne could be heard, and excerpts and arias from Mozart's operas were occasionally given.

This proved sufficient to support at least one musician of outstanding talent, WALDEMAR THRANE (1790-1828). He belonged to a wealthy family which had shown considerable interest in music; his father and two brothers were excellent performers who had also tried their hand at composition. Waldemar Thrane gave up a career in the navy and went to Paris to study music with Baillot, Reicha and Habeneck. According to contemporary reports he must have been an unusually able violinist and conductor, but it is as the composer of the first Norwegian musical comedy that he has secured for himself a niche in the nation's musical history. *Fjeldeventyret* (Adventure in the Mountains) is a naive, but charming, comedy written by the poet Bjerregaard in 1824 and performed in Oslo with Thrane's music in February, 1825. Since that time it has been given fairly often, the last time in 1948, and among the singers who have taken the leading soprano part is Kirsten Flagstad.

Fjeldeventyret is in the style of the French *opéra comique,* which was then at the height of its success, and its fresh and pleasant music reminds one of Boïeldieu. The arias seem to prove that however feeble musical life must have been in Oslo at that time, there were at least well trained singers who could be relied upon to produce the most difficult coloratura parts. But Thrane's opera would scarcely have been repeated so often, were it not for one particular number, *Aagot's Song,* which is one of the most beautiful melodies in Norwegian music before Grieg. Sung by a peasant girl, it has a distinctly national flavour. Thrane must have listened intently to folk music, to the simple songs and the calls of the dairy maids, for he has caught the very spirit of Norwegian folk music years before any collection of folk music was published. *Aagot's Song* was a favourite with Jenny Lind, who delighted in the difficult leaps of the cow-call, and embellished the song with elaborate *fioratura* passages and *cadenzas.*

There is little to justify reference to other composers of the first thirty years of national independence. Some of

them were amateurs given to composing sentimental songs
for the drawing-rooms or martial hymns for patriotic occasions; others were organists who wrote cantatas for festivals
and jubilees, rather feeble efforts in a colourless classical
style reminiscent of Haydn, Mozart and the French operatic
composers.   Until 1850 Norwegian music was, with the
exception of the works by Berlin and Thrane, the music of
dilletanti, whether the composer was a professional musician or an amateur.   None of them had any solid foundation in theory or counterpoint.

Out of this *milieu* grew the first two musicians who made
composition their chief occupation : HALFDAN KJERULF
(1815-1868) and MARTIN ANDREAS UDBYE (1820-1889).
Both were originally amateurs whose great interest in music
compelled them to seek theoretical training rather late in
life.   Kjerulf was over thirty when he received his first
lessons in composition and was thirty-five when he went to
Leipzig to study at the Conservatoire.   Udbye at the age of
thirty was still a poor schoolmaster at Trondheim with,
apparently, no chance of getting a thorough musical edu-
cation.   He arrived at Leipzig in 1851, the same year in
which Kjerulf left.

Halfdan Kjerulf's musical career was launched on a
wave of musical interest in the early 1840's.   By that time
the musical life of Oslo ceased, to a large extent, to be
typically provincial.   The need for thoroughly trained
artists had increased, and several foreign musicians found it
possible to settle in Norway.   Some of them like CARL
ARNOLD (1794-1873), Kjerulf's first teacher, and FRIEDRICH
AUGUST REISSIGER (1809-1883), who wrote some excellent
compositions for male choir (for instance *Olav Trygvason*)
played a great part in Norwegian musical life.   Several
choirs were founded in the same period and subscription
concerts were started giving symphonic programmes of a
much higher standard than heretofore.

Halfdan Kjerulf's output was very limited both in quan-
tity and range.   He kept to the miniature forms, the *lied*
and the short piano piece, never wrote anything for the
orchestra or in the sonata form.   Choral works are his only
pieces requiring a large number of performers.   But though
modest and diffident, he was a master of the miniature and

wrote some of the most poetic *lieder* in the Norwegian repertoire. His retiring nature made him avoid passionate or grandiose themes; he knew that his field was the intimate poetry of Welhaven, euphonious and polished, delicately tinged with romanticism. Kjerulf had an exquisite feeling for nature and could with a few notes evoke the calm beauty of his own country, the environs of Oslo, the still forests and dark, mirror-like lakes, the fragrance of a summer's day and the haunting sweetness of a night in spring.

Kjerulf's *lieder* were mostly in stanza form; their melody is delicate, expressive and beautifully moulded and the piano accompaniment is imaginative and exquisite in texture, never mechanical and never too thick. Mendelssohn and Schumann were his models, but he had his own distinctive touch, a tinge of melancholy that revealed his resignation and his quietly reflective spirit. He was preeminently the poet of sweet memories. With all his limitations he was a master, and his best songs have an evocatory power seldom equalled in Norwegian music and only surpassed by Grieg. Although very simple and never very difficult to sing and play, they need interpreters with a fine sense of poetry and an intense feeling for the beauty of line and phrase.

Whereas Kjerulf was the pioneer in vocal music, Udbye was Norway's first instrumental composer of note. He was not afraid of tackling the large forms in chamber music and opera, but was still more hamstrung by circumstances than Kjerulf. A schoolmaster and organist in a provincial town, he was prevented by intrigues from getting the recognition and promotion he deserved; through no fault of his own he failed to occupy the place in Norwegian music that was due to him. It is no wonder that his last composition, *Ensomme Stridsmænd* (Lonely Fighters) reveals a sense of frustration and loneliness, though it must be said that a vein of sardonic humour helped him to overcome misunderstanding and neglect. While in Leipzig he wrote two string quartets brought out by German music publishers; later he composed some orchestral pieces, cantatas and other choral works, one operetta, two musical comedies and the opera *Fredkulla* (1858), which has never, however, been performed. A fire which broke out at the theatre just before the first performance in 1877, destroyed every hope of having it shown on the stage, as both the music score and the orchestral parts were lost.

Udbye was a composer of the romantic-classical school of Mendelssohn and Schumann, and with the change in taste in the late 19th century his works became well-nigh forgotten. He published only a few part songs, some *lieder* and pieces for 'cello and piano; the rest of his works exists only in manuscript. Udbye's music reveals a keen sense of instrumental colour, learnt from Mendelssohn, Weber and Marschner, and a rugged individualism which avoided lushness and sentimentality and refused to pander to popular taste.

A third composer whose name is linked with these two pioneers was LUDVIG MATHIAS LINDEMAN (1812-1887). His work, too, was of immense importance in Norwegian musical history. Lindeman was the scion of a family which, boasting many prominent musicians, could be regarded as the Norwegian equivalent of the Bach and Couperin families of Germany and France. Ludvig Mathias was the son of an organist in Trondheim who had distinguished himself in the context of a, generally, poor musical life of the times by his fine musicianship and good musical taste. In his young days—in the 1790's—he appeared publicly at concerts in Denmark and Norway as soloist in Mozart's piano concertos. All his sons received a thorough training in music, but only one of them showed real genius. Ludvig Mathias Lindeman was far ahead of his times in many respects. He was a fervent worshipper of Bach, and no other Norwegian composer could equal his knowledge and skill in counterpoint. He could turn out fugues more easily than Kjerulf could compose a song, and, for a long time, was the best teacher of theory in Oslo. In addition to this he was an outstanding organist, and his great success in London in 1871 proved that his playing was excellent judged even by international standards. He was one of the few foreign organists invited to play the new organ at the Royal Albert Hall, and his success there was followed by several concerts of his own.

It is natural that most of Lindeman's compositions—

organ pieces, choral works and hymn tunes—were written for church service. His technique was perfect and his knowledge of Protestant church music from the time of Luther to his day, without rival in Norway. His background made him an obvious choice for the job of the editor of the Norwegian Church hymn-book. Besides, he had already proved his genius by writing some of the finest chorales used in the Protestant service, tunes worthy of the German chorales of the 16th and 17th centuries. In preparing his hymn-book he was aware of the fact that since Luther's time these chorales had lost much of their free rhythm, but was opposed to restoring them to their original form. Instead he fashioned them according to what was, in his days, regarded as a form suitable for religious service. This started off a heated dispute about the correct form of chorales, an argument which persisted nearly to the present day. Lindeman's hymn-book was eventually introduced into the Norwegian Church and authorized by the State despite the protests of the purists; only in recent times has a revision of his work been made in conformity with principles expressed by his opponents.

Most of Lindeman's compositions in other fields have, unfortunately, been destroyed. In his early days he wrote a number of string quartets, some organ fantasias and a piano sonata, but they were lost, together with other manuscripts, in a fire at his home. However, those of his organ preludes and choral compositions which were published reveal his skill in counterpoint. Lindeman's musical style was not popular in his day, at least not in Norway, and his compositions were considered heavy and learned. His most important contribution to Norwegian music lies, however, in another field—in his collection of folk music. He started the publication of his unrivalled symposium of melodies and dances obtained from Norwegian peasants in 1840, and between that year and 1867 edited more than 600 numbers. Lindeman possessed a unique faculty for coaxing half-forgotten melodies out of the people; his interest overcame the inconveniences of travel in the remotest parts of the country, and his sensitive ear for the finest shades and the minutest deviations in pitch made him a reliable recorder and harmonizer of folk music. His monumental manuscript collection comprises about 2,000 numbers, and only one-third of them were printed in the various books of *Norske Fjeldmelodier* (Melodies from the Mountains) and *Norske Kjæmpeviser* (Norwegian Ballad Tunes).

Lindeman's importance in the musical life of Norway can scarcely be overestimated, especially in view of the great services which he had rendered, over a period of several decades, as teacher to a host of young musicians. There being no State school of music in Norway, he founded, with his brother, the *Musikkonservatoriet*, to this day the only college of music in Oslo. The conservatoire has been controlled by succeeding generations of Lindemans and is a private family concern even now, though it receives a State grant.

Although conditions in Norway were far from easy, all the above-mentioned composers found ample scope for their activities. Great virtuosos, however, had difficulty in adapting themselves to the parochialism of the small towns and preferred trying to make a name for themselves abroad. Artists like Ole Bull and Thomas Tellefsen spent most of their lives in the great musical centres of the world. OLE BULL (1810-1880), the greatest virtuoso in his day after Paganini, toured extensively in Italy, France, England and America and was everywhere hailed as a great magician of the violin. Although some musical critics disliked his ostentatiousness and lack of reverence for the works of the great masters, there was no doubt about his ability to move an audience either to tears by a beautiful cantilena, or to hysterics by an almost pyrotechnical display of trills, harmonics and double stops. His own compositions were all written to emphasize his technique and are of little value with the exception of one or two beautiful melodies which have now become popular folk songs of Norway. One of these, *Sæterjentens söndag* (Solitude of the Mountains) exists in a fine arrangement for string orchestra by Johan Svendsen.

The pianist THOMAS TELLEFSEN (1823-1874) had none of Ole Bull's arresting and egocentric personality, vitality or flair for publicity, but was a finer musician. Although he is scarcely a name now, even in Norway, he was, in his time, considered one of the greatest pianists living in Paris, and the title pages of his compositions sparkled with the princely titles of his friends and benefactors. From comparatively humble beginnings—he was the son of an organist in Trondheim—he plunged into the hectic life of Paris in the 1840's, became a pupil and intimate friend of Chopin and was accepted in the highest society circles of the French capital. The affinity of his music with Chopin's may be due to the influence of a greater personality on a smaller, but may also be explained by the close affinity between Norwegian and Polish music. The Lydian mode is prevalent in both, and the *mazurka* rhythms have their exact equivalents in Norwegian dance music. Nevertheless, Tellefsen's piano pieces have a quality of their own, especially the early ones, when the Norwegian dances he had heard and played in his youth were still ringing in his ears. His music strikes one by its vital rhythms; harmonically it is more in the traditional style, though once in a while he emulates his master's extreme chromaticism. The greater part of his output is made up of piano pieces : two concertos, two sonatas (one for two hands and one for four), *mazurkas,* waltzes, nocturnes, Norwegian dances, etc. He also wrote two violin sonatas, a 'cello sonata, a few smaller pieces for violin or 'cello with piano accompaniment, and a beautiful trio for piano, violin and 'cello. Considering its artistic qualities and aristocratic reserve, his music did not deserve the neglect into which it had fallen.

Although up to that time Bull and Tellefsen were the only Norwegian musicians to become famous abroad, it would not be fair to overlook the flutist OLUF SVENDSEN (or SVENSEN) (1832-1888), one of the best musicians of his time, who after settling in London, became a member of Queen Victoria's private orchestra and a professor at the Royal College of Music.

CHAPTER 3

THE GENERATION OF GRIEG
AND SVENDSEN

IT IS UNDERSTANDABLE that with Kjerulf,
Udbye and Lindeman active at home and Ole Bull
and Tellefsen voyaging abroad as the country's
musical ambassadors, national self-confidence had
received a substantial boost. Moreover, Norwegian
musical life was firmly set on its feet and the ground
prepared for the flourishing 1870's and 1880's. The
national revival of the forties and fifties made the Norwegians conscious of their national heritage : of their old
fairy tales published by Asbjörnsen and Moe and recog-
nised as masterpieces of story-telling, of their folk ballads
collected and edited by Landstad and their folk music
published by Lindeman. A national school of art led by
J. C. Dahl and Th. Fearnley, and later by Tidemand and
Gude, discovered the Norwegian landscape and made Norwegian scenery and folklore the subject of their paintings;
poets like Welhaven began to use Norwegian legends as
literary raw material. The sixties and seventies saw the
emergence of one great artist after another, of dramatists
like Henrik Ibsen and Björnson, novelists like Jonas Lie,
painters like Fritz Thaulow, Erik Werenskiold and Christian
Krohg. Composers like Edvard Grieg and Johan Svendsen
fitted well in the pattern of this great awakening of Norwegian art.

It is surprising how many Norwegian composers were
born around 1840. Winter-Hjelm was born in 1837,
Svendsen in 1840, Lammers in 1841, Nordraak and Neupert
in 1842, Grieg in 1843, Selmer in 1844, Cappelen in 1845,
Haarklou and Agathe Backer Gröndahl in 1847, Ole Olsen
and Holter in 1850. These were the men and women who
created the Norwegian music of the 1870's and 1880's,
supported by artists like Erika (Lie) Nissen, Gudbrand Böhn,

Hans Nilsen and J. Hennum. Never since has Norway experienced a growth of musical comprehension as extensive as that of the days of the public awakening to the great music of past and present ages. An orchestra approaching Continental standards was built up, choral societies capable of performing great works started, the masterpieces of Bach and Beethoven produced, and Richard Wagner introduced by enterprising conductors.

The oldest of the new generation of composers was OTTO WINTER-HJELM (1837-1921), who came back from his studies in Leipzig and Berlin in 1863 and started his long career as composer, critic, conductor, organist and teacher of singing, piano, organ and harmony. It was in the latter capacity that he had rendered his greatest service to Norwegian music. Although the school he founded together with Grieg proved of short duration, he successfully continued his private lessons. With the background of a very extensive theoretical knowledge he proved to be an excellent teacher. He also edited a valuable piano and organ school. In 1863 he took over the conductorship of the philharmonic concerts, but had to give it up in 1871 on account of personal and financial difficulties. His work in this sphere was carried on by Grieg and Svendsen. As a music critic he was a staunch defender of Mozart and Mendelssohn and attacked violently modern composers like Wagner and Richard Strauss. Because of this he soon became something of a bogey to the new generation, and it was difficult for his contemporaries to give a just appreciation of his works. Reaching the venerable age of ninety-four, he came to be regarded by the younger musicians as hopelessly out of date and his compositions were forgotten in his own lifetime.

Winter-Hjelm never ventured far from the classic-romantic style inculcated in him at the Leipzig conservatoire; his songs and piano pieces were mostly simple works in the Mendelssohnian manner. They are tuneful and with a strong national flavour, and one of his songs, at least, has become a folk song. His two symphonies deserve mention because they were the first symphonies to be written in Norway (with the exception of those by Johan Heinrich Berlin); naturally enough they are reminiscent of Mendelssohn and Gade, but have a decided Norwegian character. One of them incorporated an authentic folk song as a theme. His best compositions were the large choral works, the *Luther Cantata* of 1883, *Torbjörn Kolbrunarskald* with its splendid double choirs, and the cantata *Lyset* (The Light), written for the University of Oslo to words by Björnson and first performed in 1911.

Equally faithful to the Mendelssohnian tradition was CHRISTIAN CAPPELEN (1846-1916), who came to Leipzig as early as 1860. Cappelen was a modest and retiring musician who never excited any controversy. As an organist he was without peer in Norway, and it was only natural that he should have succeeded Lindeman at *Vaar Frelsers* (Our Saviour's) Church in Oslo. Although he gave many concerts in Norway, he never went abroad in spite of invitations from Paris and America. His fine craftsmanship is evident in his compositions, mostly religious works, cantatas and other choral works, hymns and organ pieces. Bach and Mendelssohn were the models he used for his organ preludes, fantasias, songs and motets.

At that time Leipzig, the musical capital* of the Continent, attracted many talents from Scandinavia. Most Norwegian musicians of the 19th century were, in fact, trained there and imbibed the spirit of Mendelssohn and Schumann. This contributed to the fact that Norwegian music of the second half of the 19th century was strongly influenced by German romanticism. But to make Norway's music its own, to lift it above the level of imitations of German models, there was need for originality and genius. That came with the music of Nordraak and Grieg.

RICHARD NORDRAAK (1842-1866) died before he could fulfil the promise he gave by his songs and piano pieces, but he will always be remembered in the history of Norwegian music for the incentive he gave to Grieg. He received his musical training in Copenhagen and Berlin, but like his cousin, Björnstjerne Björnson, was filled with a desire to create a national art. It was his infectious enthusiasm that roused in Grieg the wish to carry Norwegian music beyond

---

* The only rival to Leipzig's fame was Berlin where the standard of teaching was not, however, very different.

the vague Nordic romanticism which was the ideal taught by the Mendelssohn-inspired Gade. Nordraak's own compositions have a strong personal touch, a manly strength coupled with rich sensuousness, and some of his songs have remained popular to the present day. He was also the composer of the national anthem, and would therefore be remembered even if he had written nothing else.

When Nordraak died at the age of only twenty-four, EDVARD HAGERUP GRIEG (1843-1907) felt that the responsibility for realising Nordraak's dreams had fallen to him. Spurred on by his colleague he had struck out boldly along a road which seemed dangerous to the cautious Gade. Grieg's early songs and piano pieces are in Gade's romantic vein, but some of them, like the well-known *I Love You*, show an extraordinary gift of melody and a tendency towards unorthodox harmonies. The personal touch is still stronger in the piano sonata in E minor and the first violin sonata (in F major, op. 8); the latter incorporates a *springdans* which, with its strong Norwegian character, its wild rhythm and open fifths in the harmony must have shocked the sensibility of Gade. The piano concerto, written during his honeymoon in the lovely country of northern Zealand, in Denmark, was a step further away from Mendelssohn classicism. But only in the violin sonata in G major (op. 13) did he free himself completely to give full rein to his love of strong rhythms, unusual harmonies and melodics that owe something of their power to Norwegian folk music, but have a sweetness and freshness all of their own.

Grieg's music is so well-known that it is unnecessary to go into detail and allow him the space he would otherwise deserve in a history of Norwegian music. It must be granted, though, that his output was uneven, that he was never quite happy in the large forms, and that he used tricks of melody and harmony that may strike one as irritating mannerism. Some of his minor works have become hackneyed and his position as a great composer has been seriously challenged by critics who considered these " popular masterpieces " as inferior. But even if Grieg's music has a wider appeal than that of many a greater composer it is never sentimental, it has an outdoor freshness which is, at times, exhilarating. Grieg himself said that his music was an expression, in sounds and rhythms, of his own country, Western Norway, with its fjords and snow-capped mountains, its waterfalls and glaciers, its bleak windswept islands and sheltered valleys, its wild and desolate moors, a country ever changing from ingratiating sweetness to awe-inspiring grandeur.

Grieg was pre-eminently a composer of miniature works. His string quartet, in addition to three sonatas for violin and piano and a 'cello sonata, were his only ventures into the field of chamber music; with the exception of these and the Piano Concerto, he did not attempt any combinations of the pianoforte—his own instrument—with other instruments. He rarely wrote for the orchestra, but in the few orchestral compositions he did compose (incidental music to *Peer Gynt* and *Sigurd Jorsalfar,* two elegiac melodies for strings, symphonic dances and orchestral accompaniments to songs) he showed an original talent for instrumentation, an imaginative use of tone colour and a great understanding of the individuality of the instruments.

As a song writer Grieg must rank with the greatest. He often set music to inferior poetry and was able to create excellent compositions. But it was with his musical rendering of poems by Björnson, Ibsen, Vinje and Garborg that he achieved real greatness. For each of them he created a special style : an invigorating freshness in the Björnson songs with flowing accompaniment and bold leaps in the vocal line, and a feeling of nakedness in the Ibsen songs with poetry declaimed like a recitative over the piano's bare harmonies. He wrote finely moulded melodies to Vinje's bitter verse of wisdom, the very beauty of which is heart-rending, and imparted the intense psychological realism of his *Veslemöy* cycle of Garborg's exquisite and deply moving description of young and disappointed love.

One of his finest works is *Den bergtekne* (Der Berg-entrückte) for baritone and orchestra. A folk ballad about a man enchanted by the elves and unable to find his home again, inspired Grieg to composing one of his most intensely moving works, written, as he put it himself, " in his own heart-blood." The crowning achievements of his life were the transcriptions of Norwegian folk songs and dances for piano and the settings of four religious folk songs

for mixed choirs. With the suppleness and wildness of
their rhythms, unexpected harmonies, a mixture of tender-
ness and virile strength, the *Norwegian Slaatter* for piano
(op. 72) surpass anything written in Norway before or after.

Grieg's name will always be coupled with that of JOHAN
SVENDSEN (1840-1911), the greatest symphonic composer of
the period. Like Udbye and Tellesfen, he was of purely
Norwegian stock and was the son of a musician who had
come to Oslo from the country to play in the military band.
From his early childhood Svendsen must have heard the
traditional country dances played by his father on the
fiddle. He soon decided to follow his father's profession,
and unlimited energy and optimism contributed to his
success. He went to Germany without a penny, managed
to get accepted at the Leipzig conservatoire, and it looked
as if he had before him a promising career as a violinist. A
cramp in the hand, however, forced him to give up playing;
he was transferred to the composition class and soon made
astonishing progress. From his Leipzig years date some of
his best works, the string quartet and octet and his first
symphony (in D major op. 4). They display freshness and
originality and show a masterly handling of form as well as
knowledge of instrumentation surprising for so young a
man as he then was. There was no doubt that he would
go far. But he was not satisfied with his studies in Leipzig;
he went to France, and in the Paris of the Second Empire
made contacts which were of paramount importance in his
musical career. The gay life among Bohemians of the
Quartier Latin inspired him in his orchestral work *Carnaval
de Paris,* composed at Bayreuth in 1872. The work reveals
his acquaintance with the orchestration of Berlioz.

The war in 1870-71 cut short his stay in France; he went
to Germany, where he made the acquaintance of Wagner
and Liszt, and then returned to Norway to take up the
position of conductor of the newly-formed orchestra of
Oslo. With the exception of short trips to France and
America he lived in Norway until 1883, when he accepted
the post of conductor in Copenhagen. As a conductor
he was the most brilliant Norway has ever produced, and
his fame went far beyond the frontiers of Scandinavia. In
Denmark he was admired and respected for his integrity

and craftsmanship as well as for his unselfish labour on behalf of young Danish composers. From the very beginning of his work there he was the champion of Carl Nielsen, who represented quite a different type of music from his own.

After his transfer to Copenhagen Svendsen did not compose a single work; his third symphony never materialized. His output was accordingly very slender and contained only twenty-six opus numbers. But everything he wrote bears the mark of a sure taste and thorough workmanship. He did not strike out along new roads, but stuck to the romantic-classical style he had adopted in the sixties. Its essence was far from the diluted Mendelssohnism of so many of his contemporaries. The strong national character of his style, fascinating rhythms and imaginative orchestration gave his music a vitality which has survived the vagaries of changing tastes. In Norwegian music he remains a great classic whose orchestral works are an essential part of the national repertoire suitable for all great occasions.

The best of his productions are two symphonies, the early one in D major and the second in B flat major, a work of his more mature years. But the freshness and taste of his orchestration are equally evident in shorter works of a more popular appeal such as his four Norwegian *rhapsodies,* his *polonaises,* a *romance* for violin and orchestra, the *Romeo and Juliet* overture and his tone poem *Zorahayda.* Svendsen also wrote a violin as well as a 'cello concerto and transcriptions for the orchestra of works by Wagner and Schumann. His orchestral settings of folk songs are among the most endearing of his works.

His contemporary JOHAN SELMER (1844-1910) was, like Svendsen, pre-eminently a composer of orchestral works strongly influenced by Berlioz, Liszt and Wagner. He was the most important representative in Norwegian music of a movement known as the neo-German school. Early travels in the Mediterranean gave him a taste for the exotic, evident in his works *La Captive* for contralto and orchestra, and *La Marche des Turcs sur Athènes* for baritone, male choir and orchestra, both set to texts from Victor Hugo's *Les Orientales.* Unlike most Norwegian

Richard Nordraak (1842-1866)   Halfdan Kjerulf (1815-1868)
        Edvard Hagerup Grieg (1843-1907)
Johan Svendsen (1840-1911)   Christian Sinding (1856-1943)

Harald Sæverud (b.1897)
Ludvig Irgens Jensen (b.1894)

Klaus Egge (b.1908)
Sparre Olsen (b.1903)

composers, Selmer studied in Paris. He threw himself in the whirlpool of political activities of the city and during the Commune of 1871 became a member of the Musical Committee. One of his works, the *Scène funèbre,* was about to be performed when Government troops entered Paris and scattered the musicians. Nearly all of Selmer's music is programme music; he had to be inspired by a text or an idea. In the songs with piano or orchestral accompaniment he created his own style, a kind of recitative, somewhat reminiscent of Wagner, full of sudden modulations and changes of tempo. His aim was not to create beautiful music, but to express the text, and every inflection in the poetry is reflected by his music. He was prepared to use any means to gain the desired effect, his realism knew no limitations. He often succeeded in achieving grandiose effects by the intensity of expression, at other times his music strikes one as bizarre and far-fetched, perhaps even in bad taste. With all the sudden changes in mood and expression the whole composition is apt to fall to bits, and only rarely did he create a work which could be considered as an artistic whole.

Selmer's best works are his orchestral compositions for voice and orchestra, choir and orchestra and for the orchestra alone. His study of Berlioz, Liszt and Wagner and his intimate knowledge of the modern orchestra enabled him to secure the most striking effects. He cared little for sensuous beauty; percussion and brass interested him more than the lushness of strings, and he introduced the most curious instruments into the orchestra, including a tin pan. The *Flemish Carnival* is typical of his crass realism, irony and satire and his love of the bizarre. His earlier years were dominated by the French poets, Victor Hugo, Charles Nodier, Musset etc. and some of his most captivating works are based on their poetry. Later he discovered Shelley, wrote the symphonic poem *Alastor* and set three of his poems to song and orchestra. The greater part of his later songs are to texts by Scandinavian and German poets. The grandiose *Spirit of the North* for baritone, male choir and orchestra and *Greeting to Nidaros* for tenor, male choir and brass band are two of the happiest results of his collaboration with Norwegian versifiers.

The purely orchestral works of Selmer include, besides the *Scène funèbre* and the *Flemish Carnival,* the suite *In the Mountains,* transcriptions of two Schumann songs for strings and his most ambitious work *Prometheus.* The latter discloses all the qualities of Selmer's art, good and bad, his skilful handling of the orchestra, search for truth that knew no compromise, an ardent love of liberty and hatred of tyranny, his inclination towards the grotesque, and an inadequate power of fitting all his magnificent ideas into one coherent whole.

Representing a modernistic programme Selmer stood alone among Norwegian musicians and never became a popular composer. The general trend, meanwhile, continued along lines inaugurated by Kjerulf and followed by Svendsen viz. as a German-originated romanticism coloured with melodic and rhythmic features borrowed from Norwegian folk music. This was the style of most of the newcomers in the seventies and eighties, of Johannes Haarklou, Iver Holter and Catharinus Elling. The eldest of them, JOHANNES HAARKLOU (1847-1925), an intensely interesting figure of the Norwegian musical world, was the son of a peasant, endowed with great gifts and a consuming passion for music, as well as with tenacity and *naïveté,* he was able to overcome all difficulties and adverse criticism. Not until he was twenty-one, did he have an opportunity to hear classical music. At the age of twenty-six, he got his first chance of studying outside Norway. After spells of residence in· Leipzig and Berlin he settled in Oslo in 1880 as organist, composer, conductor and critic.

One might think that a man from one of the remotest valleys of Western Norway, familiar with folk music from childhood and brought up on folk songs and dances, was bound to be strongly influenced by them. The fact was, however, that only in his small pieces did he follow native tradition; his large works were composed according to the best precepts of the Leipzig conservatoire. Rigid formalism and an elaborate counterpoint made his symphonies and chamber music rather dull and uninspired and showing only occasional flashes of genius. Nothing could shake Haarklou's reverence for the great classical tradition, and in spite of ridicule and criticism he persisted in turning out large-scale works having little chance of being performed or published. Of his orchestral compositions the best are the Piano Concerto op. 47 and the impressive suite *In the Westminster Abbey*, written in 1899 after a visit to England.

Compared with his contemporaries Haarklou was a prolific composer; his production includes four symphonies, five operas (of which four were performed), suites, dances for the orchestra, cantatas and other choral works, chamber music, songs, piano pieces and organ works. His oratorio, *The Creation*, to words by Henrik Wergeland (first performed in 1891) was his most ambitious work; its composition took him ten years. There was one field, however, viz. that of the shorter choral composition which brought him unqualified praise from all critics. Haarklou enriched the already abundant repertoire for male choirs with some splendid works, mostly to the texts by Per Sivle and Knut Hamsun. The most important of these are *Varde* (The Beacon), *Fenrir* (The Vampire) and *Tord Foleson*. Finally, mention ought to be made of his fine compositions for organ, prelude and fugue, two symphonies, some shorter preludes and other works.

IVER HOLTER (1850-1941) rendered his greatest service to Norwegian music as an orchestral and choral conductor. For twenty-five years he conducted the symphony orchestra (*Musikforeningen*) of Oslo and at one time or another was conducting all the great male choirs of the capital. In 1897 he founded *Holters Korforening*, a mixed choir set up to perform Norwegian and foreign choral works jointly with his symphony orchestra, and was its leader until 1921.

It was no wonder that with all this work on hand he found little time for compositions; in fact, most of his works were written during summer holidays. Though he lived to the age of ninety-one, his opus numbers reached only the figure of twenty-five. Of these six were cantatas written for special occasions and with little chance of survival; the best known is *Til Fædrelandet* (To my Native Country) composed in 1895 and performed several times since then. A few piano pieces and songs, two string quartets, a symphony, a violin concerto, a suite for orchestra, a few

shorter orchestral works and a handful of choral compositions for a male quartet or a women's choir consti-
tute the rest of his output. Of the piano pieces the *No-
velletten* are the most interesting and show some striking
rhythmic and harmonic traits. Some of the songs are very
effective, especially those with orchestral accompaniment.
Of the string quartets the second in G major (op.18) is a
fine work and has been performed several times in Norway. But it was his works for the orchestra and for the
choir that gave him a prominent place among the composers of his generation. It was only natural that with
his great experience as a conductor he was able to handle
the orchestra with supreme skill. In the beautiful composition for strings entitled *St. John's Eve* or in his music
to Goethe's play *Goetz von Berlichingen* as well as in his
violin concerto we see him at the height of his power.
Holter was trained in the classic-romantic tradition of the
Leipzig conservatoire and this is reflected in the sound
workmanship of his symphony and string quartets, all of
which show an extensive use of Norwegian dance rhythms.
But Holter was more of a realist than his precursors; his
music exudes manly power, direct and unsentimental, and
is an expression of a healthy and vigorous mind. He has
more in fact in common with younger composers like
Sinding and Johan Halvorsen than with his contemporaries.

Although Catharinus Elling and Per Winge were younger
than the above mentioned composers and lived to a great
age they stuck to the romantic tradition all their lives.
Both were highly cultured men who in their works showed
an excellent taste and fine workmanship. Following his
music studies at Oslo and Leipzig and graduation in modern languages CATHARINUS ELLING (1858-1942) spent ten
years in Berlin and here most of his larger works were
written, including his Symphony in A major, a piano
quartet, two string quartets, an oratorio *Den forlorne sön*
(The Prodigal Son) and the opera *Kosakkerne* (The Cos·
saks), the latter based on Tolstoy's novel. All his works in
the sonata form are characterized by a sure sense of form,
a finely shaped melody and sound counterpoint. There is
nothing excessively emotional about them and no evidence
of a search for effect. Elling's reticence was remarkable in

a period when Wagner and Tschaikovsky were the models, and his integrity and individualism were interpreted by his critics as stubbornness.

Elling's conservatism was especially noticeable in his orchestral works.. He never tried to dazzle by unusual effects or by a magic of tone colours of modern orchestration. He deliberately stripped his works of anything that might divert attention given to line and texture. The result of this treatment was that his orchestral works became well-nigh ascetic in their renunciation of colouristic effects. This is the main reason why his symphony and his orchestral suites never met with the appreciation their fine workmanship deserved. His most popular works were the Norwegian suite, transcriptions for orchestra of folk songs and dances.

As was the case with Haarklou's work, unstinted praise was given to his choral compositions, the oratorio *The Prodigal Son,* a ballad for baritone, male choir and orchestra entitled *Kong Inge og Gregorius Dagsön* to Björnson's text, and the psalm *Ærer det evige foraar i livet* for mixed choir and orchestra (also to Björnson's words) and a host of shorter pieces such as his settings of folk songs. His compositions for song and piano have the same characteristics as his chamber music; the stress is on melody, and the harmonic progression follows closely the development of the melodic line. The construction of his songs is diametrically opposed to that of Selmer, in which every inflection of poetry is expressed in music. Elling's technique aimed at expressing the general mood of the poem, and therefore he favoured strophical composition. With his fine sense of melody he created some exquisite songs to texts by Garborg and Sivle.

This feeling for melody was of the greatest value to him in his work as collector of folk music. He started in 1898 in the remote valley of Setesdal and in the following year received a State grant to continue his work. For twenty-five years in succession he spent the summer in one or other country districts rescuing what was left of songs, hymns and dances and succeeded in noting down more than 1,400 songs of which only a small part has been printed. His harmonization of the folk music and transcrip-

tions for piano or choir show an intimate feeling for the
individuality of the Norwegian folk song, its tonal characteristics and possibilities. His numerous works on the folk
music published by the Royal Society of Sciences are
authoritative.

PER WINGE (1858-1935), though resembling Elling in the
stress he placed on melody, was a composer of a far more
modest output who chiefly kept to the small forms. The
work by which he first attracted attention was the beautiful trio for violin, cello and piano opus 3 (1883). For a
considerable length of time he was a conductor, first in
Bergen, then at the Christiania Theatre and the *Central-
teatret* in Oslo, and in this capacity wrote some stage
music and a short operetta. But it was his shorter works,
songs and piano pieces which made him famous. Winge's
songs have a charm quite of their own; he had an extraordinary gift for sweet melody, and his children's songs
are known to every Norwegian youngster.

Winge's music may be considered a continuation of
Kjerulf's, and the same applies to the compositions of
AGATHE BACKER GRÖNDAHL (1847-1907). Her work was distinguished by a purity and charm of melody as well as
aristocratic reserve. Agathe Backer Grödahl was one of
the foremost pianists of her day and it may be recalled
that G. B. Shaw wrote enthusiastic reviews of her concerts in London around 1890. Together with ERIKA (LIE)
NISSEN (1845-1903) who scored tremendous successes during
her appearances abroad, few though they were in number,
she set a remarkably high standard of piano playing in Oslo,
a fact commented on by foreign musicians visiting Norway. Both as a pianist and a composer she was extraordinarily gifted and her songs and piano pieces show remarkable resourcefulness and great inventive spirit within
the relatively narrow limits she set herself. He entire output consisted of songs and piano pieces, among them some
of the finest gems of Norwegian music. Her well-developed
taste, logic and intimate knowledge of the possibilities of
her medium ensured that anything she wrote was well
rounded and constructed; No Norwegian composer has
had her gift of revealing the poetry of the pianoforte. In
many of her compositions she anticipated impressionism

which was to reach Norway only after her death.

The third pianist of international fame was EDMUND NEUPERT (1840-1888) who spent most of his life outside Norway. He was the successor of Nicholas Rubinstein at the Moscow conservatoire and died in New York, where he settled as a teacher, succeeding at the same time in creating a deep impression by his playing. His compositions for the piano were mainly studies and drawing-room pieces.

Yet another of Norway's artists who ought to be mentioned in a survey of the country's musical history is THORVALD LAMMERS (1841-1922), a baritone of a fine voice and taste in interpretation. He was the founder, in 1881, of the *Cæciliaforeningen,* the first mixed choir in Oslo. His performances of classical choral works rendered a splendid service to Norwegian music. As a singer he was an inspiration to Grieg and other Norwegian composers, and the first public performance of many of their works was entrusted to him. As a composer he was known by several attractive songs and the cantata *Fred* (Peace) to words by Björnson.

It may be appropriate at this point to mention briefly PER LASSON (1859-1883), a composer of great talent whose promising career was cut short by untimely death at the age of only twenty-four. At least one of his compositions stood the test of time, though the composer himself is seldom given credit for it. It is the piano piece *Crescendo,* played all over the world in every kind of transcription.

CHAPTER 4

THE TURN OF THE CENTURY

FOR COMPOSERS active in the eighties and nineties of the last century, Grieg stood out as a great model, and his influence can be traced in the work of nearly all of them. Nonetheless, as most Norwegian composers had finished their studies in Leipzig or Berlin, Norwegian music up to World War I followed closely the trends of the German music. Germany with its rich musical culture attracted the young talent and, for practical as well as economic reasons, could be regarded as a country offering the greatest possibilities to Norwegian musicians. Thus nearly the whole repertoire of Norwegian choirs and symphony orchestras was German; furthermore as the Norwegian Lutheran Church used the same music and chorales as the German Protestant churches, it was clear that Germany could provide the best training for Norwegian organists as well as choral and orchestral conductors. Germany with her numerous opera houses also attracted Scandinavians interested in operatic techniques and provided opportunities for singers wishing to study or to take up engagements.

Of the composers mentioned in the preceding chapters only a few had any contact with non-German music. But though educated in Germany, Grieg's natural sympathies were with French rather than German music; he thought more of some of the lesser French composers like Godard, than of many of his German contemporaries, and could appreciate neither Brahms nor Reger. Selmer and Svendsen, too, were strongly attracted by French music, and especially that of Berlioz. But for the others the romantic classicism of Mendelssohn and Schumann remained a model. Fortunately they found a stronger still inspiration in Norwegian folk music, and it was in works where the national traits were most marked, in the *lied* and the part-song, that they gave of their best.

Beginning with the seventies the influence of the Mendelssohn-Schumann school, strongly entrenched at the conservatoires, began to recede. At the same time, however, the neo-German school of Liszt and Wagner started to exert an increasingly greater influence on the younger generation, and composers studying in Germany in the seventies and eighties had to take sides, for or against, the new music. Similar discussions arose in Norway, in the eighties, with the introduction at orchestral concerts of Wagner's music. In Selmer and Holter the new music found able champions among the conductors. As a composer Selmer was entirely on the side of the neo-Germans; Svendsen's later works, too, show Wagnerian traits.

From 1880 onwards one composer after another came back from Germany as enthusiastic admirers of Wagner and Liszt. OLE OLSEN (1850-1927) was the first of them. Like Svendsen and Haarklou he came of a family in which the old fiddler's tradition was kept alive; he grew up in the extreme North, and from his father he took down the Norwegian and Lapp tunes which he later used in orchestral and dramatic works. Like his contemporaries he went through the usual training at Leipzig and composed a symphony (in G major), but there his interest in classical forms ended. Instead, he turned his attention to the symphonic poem and the stage, and with works like *Asgaardsreien* and the music to Weilen's drama *Erik XIV* created a sensation in Vienna and was violently attacked by the music critic Hanslick. But his chief interest was musical drama. Being an intrepid versifier he himself wrote the text of his four operas *Stig Hvide, Lajla, Stallo* and *Klippeöerne* (The Rocky Isles). *Lajla* and *Stallo* are interesting for their treatment of Lapp themes; the former was performed with great success in Oslo in 1908 with Kaia Eide-Norena as the leading soprano. None of the other operas has been shown on the stage.

Ole Olsen scored his greatest success with his charming music to Nordahl Rolfsen's children's play *Svein Uræd,* a great popular hit and source of the immortal *Solefaldssang* (Song of Sunset). A suite from the music is a staple of the Norwegian concert halls. His orchestral music includes the symphonic poems *Asgaardsreien*—already referred to—

Alfedans (Dance of the Elves) and the *Petite suite* for piano and strings; some of his shorter choral works are still very popular and so are his numerous marches and dances written for special occasions. The greater part of his time and much of his abundant energy were taken up by his work as Inspector of Music of the Army. In this position he worked on arrangements of Norwegian works for brass band and on popularizing classical and modern music through cheap concerts given by his own military orchestra.

It will readily be understood that operatic composers had no easy time in Norway, as there was no permanent opera and only occasional performances were given by resident singers or by visiting companies from abroad. The tragic fate of SIGWARDT ASPESTRAND (1856-1941) illustrates the difficulties Norwegian composers had to contend with. Aspestrand literally starved his way through life and ended in a workhouse; of his eight operas only one, the folk opera *Sjömansbruden* (The Sailor's Bride), was performed in Norway in 1907. It was revived in 1925 with Kirsten Flagstad as the leading soloist. Although he spent thirty years in Germany and also visited England and France, he was not in the least affected by modern trends in operatic music, but kept to the tradition of Weber and Lortzing. His operas are pleasant and tuneful, but in the age of Richard Strauss and Puccini they had little chance of success.

The most important operatic composer of the age GERHARD SCHJELDERUP (1859-1933) was, on the other hand, a staunch supporter of Wagner. But he tried to avoid the latter's influence in his own works and preferred to follow Verdi instead. The fact remains that he never really managed to shake off the impression Wagner's music had made on him, and Wagnerian idioms are found in all his compositions. Schjelderup came from Bergen, Grieg's home town, and after university studies went to Paris to study 'cello and composition with Savard and Massenet. A performance of Wagner's *Niebelungen* in Karlsruhe in 1887 woke in him the desire to create a Norwegian music drama; from then on he concentrated on stage music. He set to music the play by Kristoffer Jansson *Ostenfor sol og vestenfor maane* (East of the Sun and West of the Moon). Encouraged by the conductor Felix Mottl, who was greatly interested in his music, Schjelderup wrote the operas *Sonntagsmorgen* (Munich 1893) and *Norwegische Hochzeit* or *Bruderovet* (Prague 1900). His other stage works include incidental music to Karl Gjellerup's Indian drama *Offerildene* (Sacrificial Fires) and the operas *Am heiligen Abend, Die scharlachrote Blume* (based on the *Scarlet Pimpernel*), *Sturmvögel* and *Liebesnächte*. Only a few of his numerous operas were staged, in spite of an attempt on the part of Richard Strauss, d'Albert and other German musicians to get his chief works (*Ostenfor sol og vestenfor maane* and the *Scarlet Pimpernel*) performed. Schjelderup had a high standing among musicians in Germany, where he spent most of his life. Being a writer as well as musician (he was the author of works on Grieg and Wagner and co-editor of the *Norsk Musikhistorie*) he wrote the texts of his operas himself. Both operas and his orchestral works (the symphonic poem *Brand,* two symphonies, suites etc.) reveal Schjelderup's intimate knowledge of the modern orchestra and his skill and imagination in handling it.

CHRISTIAN SINDING (1856-1943) was equally drawn to Wagner, but avoided the temptation of yielding to his influence by concentrating on instrumental and chamber music, the symphony and the concerto. He composed only one opera, *Der heilige Berg,* performed at Dessau, in Germany, in 1914. No one, since Grieg and Svendsen, had played a greater part in Norwegian musical life than Sinding, who for the last thirty-five years of his life was acknowledged as leader of Norwegian composers. From the time he attracted public attention by his piano quintet in 1885, he was acclaimed as one of the greatest musical geniuses of the day. Despite hostility of some critics and of a part of the public he succeeded, in his own lifetime, in becoming a venerated classic.

Sinding was less consciously nationalistic than his immediate precursors, but his works have all an unmistakeable Nordic flavour. Like Richard Strauss he may be termed a romantic realist. He often selected his themes in remote ages or far-off countries, but there is nothing

dreamlike about his music, even when it tries to conjure
up the world of a medieval ballad. His music radiates
energy and his symphonies and concertos stage fierce
battles with triumphal outcomes. There was no sentimentality about Sinding, and he never sought sensuous beauty
for its own sake. At times his music may sound harsh and
strident, and the public of the eighties certainly found it
so. His piano quintet with its succession of fifths roused
the critics, both in Germany and Norway, to a fury. But
in his youthful vigour he never took it to heart; he threw
Mendelssohnian eclecticism to the winds and exposed its
supporters to ridicule.

Of Sinding's extensive output the greater part is represented by instrumental works. Besides a large number of
smaller works for piano, and piano and violin he wrote
several violin suites and sonatas, a piano quartet, a
string quartet and a piano quintet. The latter is one of
the landmarks of Norwegian chamber music, and though
its daring novelties do not shock anybody nowadays, it
still delights by its forceful vigour. The early Piano Concerto (opus 6) continues to be one of the concert favourites,
the Violin Concerto is also played and his three symphonies are part of the stock repertoire of Norwegian
symphony orchestras.

The new in Sinding's orchestral and chamber music
was unorthodox harmony, clashing counterpoint and extreme thickness of texture, sometimes resulting in an over-
whelming sonority, but sometimes also capable of pro-
ducing just a muddle. His piano works are notable for
the richness of sound produced by doubling of parts in
fifths and octaves; some of the accompaniments to the
songs are nearly orchestral. Orchestra-like massiveness
found in the combination of the piano with the string
quartet inspired him to compose one of his most characteristic works.

That Sinding could also be an intimate poet is shown
by his fine songs. The freshness and naturalness of his
melodies and the effectiveness of the piano accompaniment made them favourites both in homes and concert
halls. Some of them are real gems in their perfect marriage
of words and music, and to this group belong the settings

to the neo-romantic poets J. P. Jacobsen, Holger Drachman and Vilhelm Krag.

It was only natural that Sinding should feel closely attached to Germany and to German culture. He studied in Leipzig and scored some of his greatest successes there. Felix Weingartner had conducted the first performances of his symphonies, German critics acclaimed him as the great exponent of the Nordic spirit and his only opera was written to a German text. To Sinding, Germany stood for culture and civilisation, and when the Germans invaded Norway in 1940, the octogenarian composer who was deaf and, in effect, cut off from the outside world, let himself be used by German propaganda. Sinding's popularity suffered and his music was quietly boycotted by the Norwegians; only recently have his works re-appeared in the programmes of public concerts.

A combination of classical forms with instrumentation, harmony and technique of composition acquired from Grieg and the neo-German school, was characteristic of several composers of this generation. Apart from Sinding the leading musician coming under this definition was JOHAN HALVORSEN (1864-1935) who with his great gifts as a conductor, his skill in instrumentation and the handling of big forms may well be regarded as heir to Svendsen. A pupil of Brodsky and Thomson and an unusually able violinist, he was for a year leader of the Aberdeen Orchestra and then became professor at the Helsingfors conservatoire, before being appointed conductor at Bergen. In 1899 he became conductor at the newly established National Theatre of Oslo, and for a generation the Norwegian capital could enjoy his great gifts as orchestral and operatic conductor. In this capacity he led the first performance of a large number of Norwegian and foreign works. His wide activities did not leave him much time for composing, but being an extraordinarily rapid worker, he could, in a surprisingly short time, jot down music required for a given performance. Some of this work has proved to be of enduring value.

Halvorsen's musical style was chiefly derived from Grieg and Svendsen and was coupled with an effective and imaginative instrumentation. With his extensive knowledge of the Norwegian *slaatter*—he collected and published several books of Norwegian dances—he was perfectly at home in the national idiom. His music for the play *Fossegrimen* and the dances for violin and orchestra have the tang and vitality of genuine folk dances. He could also give his compositions an alluring oriental flavour as in the music to *Vasantasena* and the dances for *Queen Tamar*; and in the music to Holberg's plays—the *Mascarade* music and the *Suite Ancienne*—he wrote delightful pastiches in the style of the baroque. Halvorsen's extraordinary versatility, his masterly handling of form and his healthy vigour make him one of the most attractive of Norwegian composers. His music is always fresh, he never becomes sentimental like so many of his contemporaries. In his sixties he surprised the public by writing three symphonies which, like the works of Svendsen and Sinding, have become a part of the Norwegian national repertoire. Internationally he is known by the breath-taking march *The Entry of the Boyars* and the beautiful *Passacaglia* for violin and viola.

SIGURD LIE (1871-1904) died of consumption at the age of thirty-three, but by the time of his death had already produced works which will for ever ensure him a high place among Norwegian composers. The nephew of the great mathematician Sophus Lie, he showed equally great gifts in mathematics and music, and it looked as if he had a brilliant career before him as a scientist when suddenly he decided to devote himself to music. In spite of his activities as a choral and orchestral conductor he found time to write a symphony (in A minor), a piano quintet, a string quartet, a *Konzertstück* for violin and orchestra and a violin sonata, besides numerous songs, some piano pieces and choral works and Norwegian dances for violin and piano. There is the same healthy vigour about his music as in that of Johan Halvorsen, and he had an unusual gift of humour revealed in some of his delightful songs for male choir. His imagination and the wide range of his talent are best seen in his fine songs to texts by Helge Rode, I. Handagard, Per Sivle, Nils Collett Vogt and Vilhelm Krag; one of them, *Sne* (Snow) has become world famous. Sigurd Lie deligths constantly by the freshness of his invention, by unexpected twists in melody or harmony and by his natural declamation of poetry. In the exuberance of his wit he had scarcely an equal among Norwegian composers, and the outdoor freshness of his music has the exhilarating quality of a Norwegian spring.

If Sinding, Halvorsen and Lie may be said to have been the successors of Grieg and Svendsen, HJALMAR BORGSTRÖM (1864-1925) was the disciple of Selmer. He heard Selmer's music as a boy of fifteen and it made on him an indelible impression; like Selmer he went his own way and became one of the most original figures in Norwegian music. To him music was not to be governed by esthetic rules only, it was an expression of man's noblest thoughts and aspirations. The Leipzig conservatoire gave him little, if anything, but during his long stay in Germany from 1887 to 1901 his mind and his musical style slowly matured until he arrived at his own, personal idiom. His symphonic poem *Hamlet* for piano and orchestra, dedicated to and played by Busoni in 1903, made a great impression both in Germany and Norway. This work was followed by the symphonic poem *Jesus in Gethsemane,* a symphonic introduction to Ibsen's play *John Gabriel Borkman,* a piano concerto and a violin sonata. His crowning achievement was the vast symphonic poem *Tanken* (The Idea, 1917). In it he tried to picture the Idea as an element existing freely in space, taking its abode in man and giving him the comfort of idealism, then twisted by Mephisto into a caricature of itself and returning to space to its original form. This work, grand both in conception and form, was written with a mastery of orchestration never equalled in Norwegian music. Moreover, the composer was able to construct a satisfactory formal pattern. His last important work was the piano quintet in F major (1919) remarkable for sonority and skilful use of the instruments.

Borgström's songs are notable for the close harmony of poetry and music and the originality of both accompaniment and vocal line. Written to texts by Murad Effendi, Nils Collett Vogt, Th. Caspari and Cally Monrad they span a remarkably wide scale of emotions. But Borgström was a solitary and lonely figure in Norwegian music. He was one of the best music critics the country produced.

Although possessing his own ideas about the relative values of the absolute and programme music, he was always scrupulously fair and was widely respected for his integrity.

The type of music created by Grieg in his songs and piano pieces was a model for a large number of composers who largely confined themselves to the small forms. The most gifted of them was EYVIND ALNÆS (1872-1932) whose fine songs in the traditional late-romantic style are among the most effective and popular in the Norwegian repertoire. Being an excellent organist he was the successor to Cappelen at the *Vaar Frelsers* Church and played a great part in the preparation of the modern edition of the Norwegian hymn-book (*Koralbok for den norske kirke*). Although his large works, the piano concerto and symphony in D major (No. 2), stand out by their melodiousness, it is as a song writer that he had earned a place in Norwegian music. His beautiful melodies, eminently suitable for singing, and the sonorous and effective piano accompaniments made him famous at home and abroad.

Tunefulness is the chief characteristic of the music of JOHAN BACKER LUNDE (1874-   ), the nephew of Agathe Backer Gröndahl. He won popularity by many charming songs and some short character pieces for orchestra or for piano. A good pianist himself, Lunde often appeared at concerts in England where his songs to English texts may still be remembered.

SIGNE LUND (1868-   ), after Agathe Backer Gröndahl, the leading female composer of Norway has also been strongly influenced by Grieg. She spent many years in America and in 1917 won a prize for her composition *The Road to France* in a competition arranged by the National Arts Club. She was trained as a pianist and has written a number of very attractive piano pieces. Another instrumental composer who ought to be mentioned is GUSTAV LANGE (1861-1939). One of Norway's leading violinists, he was also one of the best teachers of harmony and violin, and most of the younger Norwegian musicians had either been his pupils or had studied his text-books. His compositions include some melodious and effective violin pieces.

The list of minor composers of this period includes two

military musicians, who as country lads received their musical training in the army. One of them, FREDRIK VILHELM GOMNÆS (1868-1925), achieved great success with his symphony in A minor (1904) performed a number of times in Oslo; he also wrote songs for male choir, a double fugue for organ and marches for military band. The other, OLE HJELLEMO (1873-1938), came from a family in which the fiddler's tradition of northern Gudbrandsdal was strong; his own compositions reflect many features of folk dance music. In addition to three symphonies he wrote a number of dances for orchestra (*Springleik, Spelmannsferd,* etc.), a suite for orchestra and a violin concerto.

Two composers of this generation, Andersen-Wingar and Gaston Borch had, thanks to their studies in France, established strong ties with French music. ALFRED ANDERSEN-WINGAR (1869-   ), a pupil of Massenet and Gedalge, is an excellent orchestrator and composer of striking orchestral works such as *Rapsodie indienne,* the *Dionysos* suite, *The Naïades* and the incidental music to the play *Iraka.* His other works include five symphonies, two violin concertos, a ballet and two operas. GASTON BORCH (1871-1926) was half French and spent most of his life outside Norway. For a long time he was conductor in Pittsburgh, St. Louis and Boston; as guest conductor he also visited many European countries. A pupil of Massenet and Johan Svendsen, he wrote several symphonic poems, *Geneviève de Paris* (performed in Paris in 1906), *Quo vadis* (Philadelphia, 1909), some orchestral suites and a number of songs and *salon* pieces. Jointly with Silvio he wrote, in 1897, a sequel to Mascagni's *Cavalleria rusticana.* HALFDAN JEBE (1868-1937) is another Norwegian composer to spend most of his life abroad. He became a professor at the conservatoire of Mexico and wrote several operas and ballets on Mexican themes. Symphonic suites drawn from them include *La ardilla, Dignidad Maya, Loltun, La mano roja,* etc.

Some of the present-day composers fit well into the pattern of musical developments described in this chapter, mainly because their work does not, in any material degree, break with the traditions of the past. One may mention here REIDAR BRÖGGER (1886-   ) who has written

some fine songs and piano pieces; GUNNAR GJERSTRÖM
(1891-   ) who attracted attention by his piano concerto of 1930 and who has also written several other piano
works, songs and choral pieces; FRIDTJOF BACKER-GRÖNDAHL
(1885-   ) best known as an eminent pianist, but also
active as a composer with some songs and piano pieces to
his credit and ANDREAS HAARKLOU (1896-   ), the son of
Johannes Haarklou, and composer of two violin sonatas,
songs and shorter orchestral works.

HALFDAN CLEVE (1879-   ) was one of Norway's finest
pianists. After studies in Berlin under Philip and Xaver
Scharwenka he settled in Oslo as a composer and pianist,
while his wife Berit Winderen Cleve, also a gifted pianist,
has gained fame as an interpreter of her husband's music.
Cleve's intimate knowledge of the instrument has helped
him to write some of the most poetic music for the piano
since Grieg and Agathe Backer Gröndahl. He owes a great
deal to Grieg and Chopin, a fact suggested by the titles :
ballades, preludes, lyrical pieces and humoresques, but his
sonorous and effective music reveals a distinctive personality. Besides shorter pieces he has written five piano concertos, a few songs with orchestra, a violin sonata and
some short orchestral pieces.

SVERRE JORDAN (1889-   ) has played, as a conductor
and critic, a leading part in the musical life of his home
town Bergen; as a composer he is best known by his numerous songs with piano accompaniment, some of them
real masterpieces. Until recently he has kept within the
bounds of tonality, but the best of his music, though written in a traditional late romantic style, has an arresting
vigour and manly audacity which gives zest to his colourful
descriptive piano and orchestral writing. Besides songs and
orchestral suites he has written several shorter choral compositions, piano and violin pieces, a musical setting to
Hamsun's *Feberdigte* for recitation and orchestra, a piano
concerto and a 'cello concerto.

Nor has ARNE EGGEN (1881-   ) ventured far beyond
the traditional style, but his close connection with the post-
war nationalist movement has won him a place among
the most prominent contemporary composers of Norway.
He was one of the few composers who could effect a

change in the national style created by Grieg and at the same time use an intensely personal idiom in songs, piano pieces, violin sonatas and choral compositions. His music reflects a tendency noticeable among modern Norwegian composers towards a more modal style of writing and away from traditional classical harmony. Only rarely, as in the *Chaconne* for organ (re-written for orchestra) does he take up a polyphonic style. His greatest works are in the field of vocal music, the choral works *Mjösen* (Lake Mjösa), a cantata for the St. Olav jubilee of 1930 (*Kong Olav*) and the opera *Olav Liljekrans*. The latter, founded on one of Ibsen's earliest plays is, except for Irgens Jensen's dramatic symphony, the only Norwegian opera produced in the last twenty-five years. At its first performance in 1940 it was hailed as the greatest Norwegian work for the lyric stage. Eggen's music has greater affinities with Norwegian folk music than that of most of his contemporaries and predecessors.

CHAPTER 5

MODERN MUSIC

A STUDENT OF NORWEGIAN music after 1920 is likely to be struck by the slenderness of links between Norwegian composers and the main Continental trends. In the inter-war period few musicians went abroad for their studies, and only for shorter periods. Berlin and Leipzig no longer had the attraction they possessed in the second half of the 19th century. Moreover the post-war days saw the rise of a school of composers in open revolt against German music.

There is no reason to assume, however, that it was a case of Norwegian musicians transferring their allegiance to France, whose stature in the field of music rose immensely since 1900. In fact, only a few composers had the advantage of a direct contact with the stimulating atmosphere of the French capital; to many, financial and linguistic difficulties presented an insuperable obstacle.

Consequently French impressionism had little influence on modern Norwegian music despite the closer affinity of Grieg's music with French rather than German taste and temperament. Between 1860 and 1910 German ideas pervaded Norwegian music to a saturation point, with the result that to most Norwegian musicians and critics French impressionism sounded vague and superficial. Nor has Russian music, apart from Tchaikovsky, had any influence in Norway, though the oriental music of Johan Halvorsen is akin to that of Borodin and Rimsky-Korsakov. Thus of the modern Norwegian composers only a few have, to any great extent, been inspired by French music and then only for shorter periods.

No one comes nearer to French impressionism than ALF HURUM (1882-   ) in his piano music. Like most of his contemporaries Hurum started as a follower of Grieg whose influence is noticeable in his excellent violin sonatas. But studies in France and in Russia (under Maximilian Steinberg) directed his attention to modern trends in music. He wrote a large number of beautiful songs and some delicate piano pieces with an exotic or fairy-land atmosphere. With his great choral composition *Lilja* (for male choir) and the symphonic poem *Bendik og Aarolilja* he turned his attention to medieval Norway; in these works and in his symphony his style is more influenced by national music. In 1929 he left for Honolulu to direct a symphony orchestra there, and with a short interruption has lived in Hawaii ever since.

In his well-known orchestral composition *Lotusland* ARVID KLEVEN (1899-1929) was strongly influenced by the French music. The modernism of his work, first performed in 1922, created quite a sensation in musical circles. Kleven's promising career was cut short by an early death, but he had already struck out on new roads where the public had difficulty in following him. His orchestral compositions include also *Skogen* (The Forest), two aquarelles to poems by Verlaine and Wildenwey, a *Symphonic Fantasia* and *Sinfonia libera*.

Another writer who began his career employing impressionist technique is BJARNE BRUSTAD (1895-   ), now one of Norway's leading composers. His early compositions like the *Suite for orchestra* (1921) dazzled by their brilliant instrumentation and were characterized by an extraordinary concentration. Later compositions, the symphonic poem *Atlantis* and two violin concertos, confirmed Brustad's reputation as an able orchestrator. The most interesting work of his early period are the *Capricci* for violin and viola (1932) marked by striking bi-tonal effects. In his *Rhapsody* for violin and orchestra (1934) Brustad turned to folk music, and in his later compositions has often tried to combine modernism with Norwegian folklore. Very few of his works have been published, but some of them were performed at international music festivals. Among his later works are a sonata for violin solo, a suite for viola solo, a divertimento for violin solo (*Pezzi atonale*), a trio for violin, viola and clarinet, the *Fanitull* suite for violin solo, a serenade for violin, clarinet and bassoon, and the opera *Atlantis*.

No one has remained more faithfully attached to French

culture than PAULINE HALL (1890-) Norway's present-day leading female composer. She is best known for her *Verlaine suite* and her *Pictures of a Circus,* both written for an orchestra. She also wrote a suite for five wind instruments (first performed in 1945), a sonata for string quartet and incidental music for several plays (*The Taming of the Shrew, Julius Cæsar, Lysistrata*). Her music is eminently French in its crispness, refinement and avoidance of sentimentality. As a music critic she has alternately delighted and infuriated musicians and public alike by the keen shafts of her brilliant criticism.

Atonality has rarely tempted Norwegian composers to deviate from the beaten path; only one of them, FARTEIN VALEN (1887-), one of the greatest men of Norwegian music, has really understood its principles and applied them consistently. From his boyhood he has been an ardent worshipper of Bach, and his own development was a logical result of his pre-occupation with polyphony. He studied in Berlin from 1909 to 1914, and his first compositions, a piano sonata and a violin sonata were written in the late romantic, extremely chromatic, style characteristic of so many Continental composers in the decade before 1914. World War I cut short his stay in Berlin, and he returned to Norway, to settle at home permanently. Since then he went abroad only for two brief visits to Rome in 1922 and to the island of Mallorca in 1932. Since 1938 he has lived on his family farm in Western Norway interested only in composition and the tending of his rose garden.

From the violin sonata op.3 one can follow his slow and painful development away from the tonality of the *Ave Maria* for soprano and orchestra, the piano trio and the Goethe songs to the free polyphonic style of the *Chinese Lyrics* op.8. Supported only by a few admiring pupils he continued along the thorny path of a musical innovator presenting, at rare intervals, such works as *Pastorale, Sonetto di Michelangelo, Cantico di ringraziamento, Le cimetière marin* (all orchestral pieces), and motets for female and male choirs. Since he settled in Western Norway, however, a surprisingly large flow of compositions came from the pen of this meticulous and critical composer : three symphonies, one violin concerto, an orchestral piece entitled *Ode to Solitude,* a serenade for five wind instruments, *La noche oscura del Alma,* a work for soprano and orchestra to words by Juan de la Cruz, songs, organ and piano pieces.

Valen is the most learned of modern Norwegian composers, and all his music bears the mark of his keen intellect and refined taste. Like most atonal music, Valen's compositions are characterized by extreme concentration, but the elaborate formal patterns are filled with a religiously intense emotion. His works are free from all superfluous matter, they are distillates of the purest and finest that Norwegian music can offer. Valen's deliberate linear style produced a beauty of outline resembling Chinese art in its grace and refinement; the different voices cross each other with a crispness that has nothing of the harshness of much atonal music, but sometimes produces a richly sensuous effect; and there are moments giving the impression of the stillness of a soul in mystical contemplation.

As a teacher of composition Valen gathered a large number of pupils of widely varying techniques. It is interesting to note that though all of them have profited by his great knowledge not one of them has followed his atonal technique. One of Valen's outstanding pupils was HARALD LIE (1902-1942) whose creative period comprised only the last eight years of his life. He died just as he was working on the symphony of Brucknerian dimensions, of which the *scherzo* only was finished and published as a symphonic dance. It would have been the third of his symphonies (apart from an early symphony which was destroyed); in addition to these he wrote several songs with orchestral accompaniment, including settings of two Michelangelo sonnets, and a few choral compositions. Harald Lie was one of the most original of modern Norwegian composers and refused to attach himself to any 'school'; because of his successful treatment of symphonic forms he must be regarded as one of the leading composers of the thirties.

Another of Valen's pupils is ERLING KJELLSBY (1901-) whose reputation as a composer became established in the thirties following the publication of his string quartet in A minor as well as of some songs and piano compositions. Interested chiefly in the minor forms he has written some very beautiful songs and is responsible for a number of fine transcriptions of folk music. His most important work up to date is the second string quartet in G major.

Fine workmanship is the hallmark of the music of KARL ANDERSEN (1903-   ) who with his interest in formal patterns and subtle tonal relations is closer to Valen than to the modern nationalists. Karl Andersen is the first 'cellist of the Philharmonic Orchestra of Oslo and is highly appreciated as a teacher of 'cello and harmony. His quantitatively small output includes a string quartet, a symphony for chamber orchestra, a suite for orchestra, and a trio for the flute, clarinet and 'cello.

The most significant development in Norwegian music between the wars was the emergence of a nationalist school of composers. Their leader, DAVID MONRAD JOHANSEN (1888-   ), has been known to the British public for his biography of Grieg. His view that Grieg's German training had ruined his development as a *national* composer and that elements of the German classical music and of the Norwegian folk music were irreconcilable is representative of the attitude of the nationalist school to foreign music. Monrad Johansen began as a disciple of Grieg whose influence is marked in his violin sonata, his early songs and piano pieces, but gradually developed a strong personal idiom both melodically and harmonically. The example of French impressionism may have helped him to develop a striking modal writing technique noticeable in the beautiful *Seven Songs to Texts from Ancient Folk Poetry* op. 6 and the chorale *Draumkvedet* (Vision of Heaven and Hell). These compositions as well as his masterpiece *Voluspaa* for solo voices, choir and orchestra to words from the *Eddas* seem to carry one back to remote ages by their quaint modal phrases and strange harmonic progressions. Later Monrad Johansen's outlook became more Continental and in the choral work *Ignis ardens* (1933), and his *Symphonic Fantasia* op. 21 (1937) he went back to classical forms and essayed orchestral polyphony. In 1940, under the Nazi government, Monrad Johansen became the leader of musical organisations in Norway and has since the war been serving a term of imprisonment for collaboration.

Among the younger nationalists Valen's pupil SPARRE OLSEN (1903-   ) is one of the most gifted. His music is largely tonal or modal, and he relies mostly on the effect of his beautiful and pure melody, harmonized in a most original and unorthodox way. Although he has written much instrumental music both for piano and for orchestra and a suite for flute, oboe and clarinet, it is as a vocal composer that he is most widely known and appreciated. His simple but striking songs have all the characteristics of folk music, and he has also written fine choral compositions, the most notable of them *Gneisten* (The Spark) and *Draumkvedet.*

The extreme wing of nationalists is represented by Eivind Groven and Geirr Tveitt. EIVIND GROVEN (1901-   ) comes from Telemark, where the *hardingfele* tradition is still very strong. His intimate knowledge of folk music made him an outstanding choice for the position of Director of the Folk Music Department of the Norwegian Broadcasting Service. Folk music tradition pervades his whole being and everything he has written bears its mark both in melody and harmony, in tonal colour and formal pattern. His large works are built up in the manner of the *slaatter,* a chain of variations and transformations of the same melody, and he makes his orchestra sound like a magnified *hardingfele.* All his works, especially the choral works *The Bridegroom* and *Ballade,* are full of haunting melodies and beautiful details of elaborate ornament reminding one of the work of native silversmiths. He is a staunch opponent of tempered tuning and has constructed a non-tempered piano and organ.

GEIRR TVEITT (1908-   ) is equally fanatic in his nationalism. He attracted attention by his *Preliminary Studies in the Lydian, Dorian and Phrygian modes* op. 1 and by violent disregard for all composers before Monrad Johansen, whose choral works he once described as the 'dawn of Norwegian music'. Geirr Tveitt is extraordinarily prolific and has already reached opus number 150; among his works are several piano concertos, two ballets, three operas and some large choral works, string quartets, sextets and trios. Keeping strictly to the old modes, he shows extraordinary inventiveness within the limits he has set himself.

Generally speaking, the nationalist composers have given their best in vocal music, and modern Norwegian music shows a surprising number of large-scale choral works. One of the most prominent of choral composers is THOMAS BECK (1899-   ) with his setting of Björnson's *Arnljot Gjelline* and his cantata *Höyfjellsliv* (The Mountains). The conductor OLAV KIELLAND (1901-   ), also closely linked with the nationalist school, has to his credit several orchestral compositions and a composition for tenor and orchestra *Mot Blaasnö-högdom* (In the High Mountains). MARIUS MOARITZ ULFRSTAD (1890-   ), though national- ist in outlook, stands aloof from the nationalist school. His music strikes one by the freedom of the vocal line, re- sembling a recitative. He is a prolific composer, having to his credit a large number of symphonies, concertos, and orchestral suites, but is better known for his songs and choral works.

Of composers imbued with a nationalist outlook, only two—Sæverud and Egge—have tried to combine nation- alism with modernism. HARALD SÆVERUD (1897-   ) is one of the most vital of modern Norwegian composers and has constantly made himself the centre of controversy. His first works, the *Ouvertura appasionata* and the Second Symphony, are dramatic; from the Third Symphony on- wards his music became more restrained and intellectual, more refined and more concentrated. The latter trait is demonstrated by his *Cinquanta variazioni piccole* on a theme only three bars in length. Sæverud has created a very original style representing a synthesis of the variation form of dance music and polyphonic treatment. His themes are tonal, but the criss-cross of patterns and har- monies gives an impression of coolness and acidity, some- times of dryness. Sæverud is chiefly an orchestral com- poser and his works, including seven symphonies, vari- ations, a *Canto ostinato* and symphonic dances, give the picture of an intensely individualistic composer who delights in his own caprices. Even though he may sting and shock, he holds the audience's attention by his surprising, constructive fancy and the tension of his harmony.

KLAUS EGGE (1908-   ), a pupil of Valen, has attempted reconciliation of atonal principles with the folk music tradition. He has seized on various characteristics in the dance music scales, the alternation between the Lydian mode and the major scale, and the harmonic peculiarities of the *hardingfele*. By building up chordal groups of fourths, fifths, sevenths and ninths instead of thirds, and by employing an extension of the scale (a major tetrachord with a Lydian tetrachord, for example), he obtains all the twelve tones of the chromatic scale. The themes of his thickly polyphonic music are usually modal or tonal, but he shows extraordinary freedom in his harmony. Although his music has not the clarity of a fully mature style, he is one of the most interesting of the younger composers. Never hampered by modesty, he has atttempted the most ambitious schemes. His most important works are the *Draumkvedesonata* for piano, symphony op. 17, and the Second Piano Concerto op. 21.

LUDVIG IRGENS JENSEN (1894-   ), who is largely self-taught, does not belong either to modernists or nationalists, but goes back to the polyphony of the Baroque and the 16th century. Bach and Palestrina are his ideals besides Chopin and Brahms. A number of his early songs and a violin sonata showed great promise, fulfilled eventually in the orchestral works *Theme and Variations* (1926, revised 1934) and *Passacaglia* (1928) which won a prize in the 1928 Schubert Centennial Contest. Then came the magnificent dramatic symphony *Heimferd* (King Olav's Return), a piano quintet, the choral work *Der Gott und die Bajadere* (words by Goethe), incidental music for *Driftekaren* (The Drover, by H. E. Kinck) and a symphony in D minor (1945). Irgens Jensen is one of the most sympathetic of modern Norwegian composers and his music convinces by its earnestness and formal beauty.

The period between the wars saw the rise of a whole school of church composers who modelled their work on Bach and Palestrina. PER STEENBERG (1870-1947) exerted great influence on the younger generation by his teaching of the pure Palestrina style. In his own motets and hymn arrangements one can find the gentle sweetness and archaic polyphony of the great Italian master. ARILD SANDVOLD (1895-   ) has played a great part in musical life as a choral conductor and organist at the *Vaar Frelsers* church; his great admiration for Bach is reflected in his compositions: motets, organ pieces, cantatas, etc. Sandvold is one of Norway's greatest organists and has been an inspiring teacher to a large number of younger musicians. Among the pupils of Steenberg and Sandvold there may be mentioned LUDVIG NIELSEN (1906-   ), KNUT NYSTEDT (1915-   ), CONRAD BADEN (1908-   ), AAGE MYKLEGAARD (1898-   ) and LEIF SOLBERG (1914-   ).

Of the youngest generation of, chiefly secular, composers the most promising are: ANNE-MARIE ORBECK (1911-   ), HALVARD JOHNSEN (1916-   ), FINN LUDT (1918-   ) and ARNE DÖRUMSGAARD (1921-   ). The latter is best known for his songs; Finn Ludt has written songs and music for several ballets, Anne-Marie Orbeck composed a *concertino* for piano and orchestra and had won a prize for a song cycle. Halvard Johnsen is more of an instrumental composer and has written various chamber music and orchestral works.

*   *

In considering the type of output characterising Norwegian music there is little doubt of the tremendous preponderance of vocal works. There is in Norway, as yet, little demand for instrumental music other than piano pieces. Norwegian composers—it must be remembered—have always had great difficulty in getting their orchestral and chamber music published; sometimes they had not even had the chance of hearing it performed. On the other hand, there is a very large number of choral societies whose demands most Norwegian composers (many of them choral conductors themselves) have striven to satisfy.

It is perhaps unfortunate therefore that choral works, though most representative of Norwegian musical output, should prove to 'be, because of their intimate link with the idiom of the country's poetry and its difficult language, the least suitable for presentation to foreign audiences. This, as well as the fact that stress at international music festivals is nearly always laid on instrumental music, has restricted the knowledge or appreciation by international audiences of the work of many Norwegian composers.

THE END

INDEX OF NAMES